LANDFILL

Landfill

JOHN
WEDGWOOD
CLARKE

Valley Press

First published in 2017 by Valley Press
Woodend, The Crescent, Scarborough, YO11 2PW
www.valleypressuk.com

First edition, first printing (August 2017)

ISBN 978-1-908853-84-4
Cat. no. VP0101

Cover photograph by the author.
Cover and text design by Jamie McGarry.

Printed and bound in Great Britain by
TJ International Ltd, Padstow, Cornwall.

Contents

Acknowledgements

Thanks are due to the editors and organisers of the following, in which versions of these poems first appeared: *Antigonish Reivew, Eborakon, Iota, POEM, Poetry Ireland Review, PN Review, Poetry Review, Poetry Wales, The Rialto, The North, Poetry Salzburg Review, Magma, Under Travelling Skies, Guardian online Poem-of-the-Week, National Poetry Competition prize-winner's anthology 2011, Advances in Marine Biology, Journal of Writing in Creative Practice, The Wolf.*

'Chalk' was commissioned by Wander for six benches on the Wolds Way. 'A Suite for Artificial Voices' was commissioned by The Creative Speech Technology Network. 'Greensand Way' was commissioned by Surrey Hills Arts for their *Inspiring Views* project. 'Folkestone Embarkations' was commissioned by Strange Cargo for the Sea Swim exhibition *Head Above Water*. 'Above 8' was commissioned by Invisible Dust for the exhibition *Offshore*.

The writing of this collection was greatly assisted by a Leverhulme Trust Artist's Residency and by a 'Grants for the Arts' award Arts Council, England.

Thanks also to the following for their expert advice, kindness and support: Magnus Johnson at the University of Hull; Harry Briggs and Rowena Marsden at Scarborough Borough Council; Chris Tomlinson and everyone at Yorwaste; and to James Byrne, Helen Tookey, Helen Mort, Ian Duhig, Philip Gross, Daniel Weston and Lara Goodband for reading and commenting on versions of this manuscript.

One grows to hate these things except on the dump.

WALLACE STEVENS

Think what it would mean to acknowledge and honour
all the places that support you...

VAL PLUMWOOD

Operation

When they removed my head,
wedging it beside crustaceans
on a shelf in the lab, I saw myself
differently. Daylight wandered

between me. A boy played with a car
on the sterile floor, then disappeared.
I felt a terrible longing to speak
but was no more than tree shadow

hammering the lip of a white sink.
They stitched me together, but there's
a wound in my voice. Sometimes water
in a jar will print its unutterable

veins of light, sometimes there's a room
with rows of taps and a gurney
where a boy is crawling, following
his hand, his hand on top of a car.

Dump Song

Sing, summer,
in our plastic bags,
sing tatters
in the shining buds,

a zephyr, tumour,
inflated heart,
snag and fritter
in the May.

The ground fluffs,
generators throb,
merry spin
the cowls,

our leaking sacks,
simmering blur,
mount up, crying
in the May.

Land is available for a variety of uses

þæs ofereode, þisses swa mæg
— Deor

Forecourt flash of steroidal cars.
Busy sponsored roundabout.
Local building society abandoned
new-build headquarters.

Unsponsored roundabout.
On scrambled commons a shaggy
horse. Then the abrupt hush
under tyres as the dream road

to the business park's lost plots begins,
black and perfectly marked,
streetlights like masts in an estuary,
yellow fields rolling in.

Pull over at the new bus stop,
step away from the car.
Time has yet to be tabled.
Silence's public transport arrives

and arrives in a heartbeat.
Across the road, a sofa in a field
waits for no man under clouds
the dead in their barrows followed into summer.

Renovation

The chisel stuns the brick and rings the hand.
Clink and rake. Loose mortar landslides

more and more, the arguments of rain and soot
slumping into the memory of a hearth, bird bones

and black sand. The room releases its breath.
Air sucks at the match. The way is clear between

inside and out. A dove on the chimney pot
broods in the blackened throat, the ear a nest.

Know Your Place

A Northern classroom after the war
and her hand's in the air.
She wants to try for grammar school.
Oh, the teacher smiles, *put it down.*

Next day, at the front, there's a box,
gift-wrapped, and she's called forward.
She likes 'nice things'
but can't think what she's done.

As she reaches for the gift,
the teacher grabs her wrist and squeezes.
You must open it in front of the class.
The clock cuts one moment from the next.

Should she save the wallpaper?
The outer layer reveals a lidded box.
Heat glazes her face as the class gazes
like sunlight through a magnifier

at her fingernails. Inside, she finds
another box, string-tied, the paper
fingernail creased. She picks at the knot
as she will always pick at the knot,

her nails bitten to the quick.
There's only another, brown paper this time,
the paper of dispatch and back office,
of shop counter and bags

of seconds, minutes, hours, clocks and klaxons –
open it, it's yours, the teacher urges.
Inside the box is nothing, and inside nothing
another box, in which she prays.

Resource Recovery Centre

I. WHO HAVE WE HERE

He was hanging around the railway bridge
torn between one side and the other.
We thought, *he's a jumper.* Just a boy really,
distracted, in a world of his own.
He came to the fence like the ghost of a prisoner,
as if saying goodbye to the space
between waste oil and the lighting locker.
We called to him through the chain-link
but he shied off back up the access road,
past the fly-tipped mattress, the drawers
without a chest, a blister pack's edge
finning through raw clay. Turned out
it was a dry run. Came back after hours,
laid himself on the line. He was no jumper.

II. COOKERS

Press and hold for the missing spark – as if
it might turn up those larks
singing over rubble. Rainwater gleams

where the blue buds sprang
beneath that old aluminium pan,
with its holes where the handle's rivets tore away.

Sometimes it caught drips,
sometimes it was the world, a spoonful of cocoa
crumbling into milk as the window

hammered into sleet and trees,
the oven door open to warm us.
I press and hold – turn and walk through walls.

III. OTHER WHITE GOODS

How it opened like a glowing tome. Then didn't.
How ice's white lump grew
until it snapped the plastic hinge
that held the icebox door in place.

Go there now and see the drain-hole
plugged with gunk. Life on hold
leaps forward in the ten-watt light.
Silence clarifies as the pump cuts out.

IV. PHOTO ALBUMS

Poured we libations unto each the dead
— Ezra Pound

So many gather in the pause
before she clicks open the case
and they burst like pigeons
from squares of sugar paper,

eyes homing now on nowhere,
lit for the last time as they fall
between bed frames, broken tiles.
Sealed against wet melamine,

faces fly on in the dark
over streets where their names
were called, gossip of whereabouts
unravelling in fields, river mist,

lights at the coast, their loneliness
now like rain falling through
distances they once gazed into –
Lights out – Incoming mattress!

V. OPERATIVE

Dan, Dan, you're Orpheus, man. Inexactly,
but enough for me, going in after photos
and letters, unable to believe they won't
have second thoughts and return

before the rain. But you should know, Dan,
you see them – every hour, every day – walk away, Dan,
with the weight off their minds, the faces
they couldn't name, such a drag, accusation – the future, Dan.

VI. PRESENCES OF NATURE

Glass slabs and weary plastic piled head-high
show the same sun differently grey,
a void transmission. Rain
glints on the circlet of an aerial:
grave goods without a body, years of on/off
dirt-halo pushbutton and sensor.

It had to go, took up too much room,
a bulky thing, that when it went
left dents in the carpet, a mini lawn
of dust and hair beneath its stand.
The room seemed strange,
like someone else's for a day or two.

The new picture's many millions of colours,
smoke's like really there, lampblack,
a hint of crow, plastic drooling
as they poke the puddled carcasses
of monitor and screen, smiling for the camera,
the dead tree's shadow sharp as you like.

VII. BUILDING MATERIALS

Hurl it in like everything they ever told you not to do
and hear the big skip's rolling emptiness
stabbed and streaked by letting go,
its steel void thronged by what passes.

It's your time and no one counts the cost.
Go for the old sash window in the corner,
savour aim gone home without consequence,
glass burst into space, your hand renewed.

VIII. ONCE IT'S IN THE SKIP THEY THINK IT DISAPPEARS

after Ted Hughes' poem 'Amulet'

Under a bedstead a filing cabinet.
Under a filing cabinet a wheelbarrow.
Over a wheelbarrow a tree in the garden.
Under the tree, four crosscut screws
secure the galvanised bucket.
Under the bucket a solid red wheel.
Around the wheel a perished tire.
Down the steps, bouncing, it booms.
Inside the bucket water collects.
Over the water, leaf-light, jet-sunder.
Suspended in water a woodlouse trembles.
Above the woodlouse, a child, breathing.

IX. MICROWAVE RADIATION

Meet me at dusk at the fluorescent-lighting locker.
We'll sort the mess of silence out,
clear the light between us
in a duel with long glass tubes,

a smashing time at no expense
but the buzz and blink of lonely sheds,
staring kitchens far beyond sleep.
How the brittle facts will burst

into broken shells, ice hushed up
a frozen beach, dead light
dissolving into dying day.
Down to the final two, we'll call an end to it,

waft them above our heads
through wheat to the pylon's foot,
moths gathering to ghost-lit hyphens
as we dowse what's lost in transmission.

X. WASTE-OIL TANK

Its black gullet swallows oil's swooping tongue,
lightness pouring up the arm.

The terminal barrel winks and gleams,
gorgeously sun-warmed like a holiday wall

under contrails unravelling
their white intestines into almost cloud.

Here is nowhere but getting there fast.
Flies hoop and dab a reservoir

of idling revs and clogged arterial roads.
Stillness in its plastic gut, like hot rails and creosote,

nostalgia chirruping. Put your ear to it:
what's that coming down the line –

River Survey

Whichever way we move,
our boots and stainless measures
set the smothering
yeast-smooth orange precipitate
smoking in the current.

Our meters say it's iron-rich as blood.
The beck bleeds a maze
of flooded wounds
past the cinema without a roof,
the shattered pub.

Autumn clarifies the space
around haw and hip,
concentrates the bent iron rod
sticking from the beck side.
Hooked from here to air,

a spider casts its shadow
speck while flies ride
sulphur-scale across
a dribbled pool, drown
above orange-frosted leaves.

Vertigo

They pulverised broken pots and querns
and mixed the temper into clay,
one body fused inside another,
old thirsts and thumbprints in new cups.

At the dream-cliff's edge, unable even to crawl,
my body's liquid flows towards
rocks surfacing like the heads of seals
in a multi-coloured plastic soup.

Small Mammal Trapping in a Field of Elephant Grass

The valley remembers its glacial lake
in fog the hillside fades into.
Sun gone white, then out,
we swerve at sudden trees
on a road with nowhere to go
but the long way round.

A pylon insists then gives up
elsewhere's ghost above
the wall of grass we're heading for.
Rut ice squeaks. Doors
slam on the dashboard
between sleep and here,

breath a place we pass through
almost lost. Hush. Quiet
consecrates the hawthorn,
an ancient church in a new estate,
its branches finned with ice,
a scintillarum of fog.

There's no way through
without blue twine
staked at the edge and running
into papery tunnels. Rime
speckles our necks as we stoop
to the traps. This one's

empty metal. This, alive,
terror teased out with straw,
mealworm, seed, into
a red-toothed shrew!
Its thousand-beats-per-minute heart
thrums in a freezer bag,

the weight of seconds.
In case we should meet again
in this vast translation,
we snip the fur on its left hind leg,
then spill it back, all sign of it
gone in a flurry of leaves.

Star Carr

I. STONEHENGE OF THE MESOLITHIC

In the shadow of the dump
a giant tractor in an empty barn,
silos, a dog off its head –
You know when you get there,
there's absolutely fuck-all to see.

Light edges mammary cloud.
Cattle trot along with a shadow
slipped through new fencing,
it can't dispel their faith
or out-sprint a turbulent pillar of flies.

Where the spear missed its mark,
where slipway timbers
turn bone-marrow soft,
where antlered headdresses
danced forests into singing water,

a poached depression, massed cattle.
It claps. The herd rears back
in comic cringe – such power
to impress, out of all proportion –
a shadow eyed by shadow beasts.

II. DEBITAGE

In the stone pieced together
from scattered flint flakes,
the blink of percussion,
shifting breath and daylight,

judgement's bone-blow
altering the fragment's trajectory
as the blade is found
in the muscle's streaming

eye and word, the body no more
than crickets leaping
before the archaeologist,
its passing known in patterns of flight.

Camping by the Mersey

We left the children for a night of wind-blown sand,
thin mats and soup from a tin.
It was nearly the memory of fun,
only harder, colder, more deliberate

in the building of the fire, that intricate house
of sticks, roots and staves from washed-up
pallets the flames hurled through
as if they might detach themselves, red insects

gnawing at the thighbone of a log,
the sand beneath sucked free of ash.
We'd made our settlement with the tide in mind
and heard it rise to the cries of curlew,

oystercatcher, the voluminous engines
of tanker and coaster, the pilot boat
sliding like a satellite among their stars.
The sand was hard and sloped towards the sea

enough to turn us over and over like the shells
we'd smashed through getting there.
That night I slept between worlds, as if I'd walked
across the beach and found a sea-lit chalet

sand drifted across the floors, walls thin
as tracing paper, eardrums, and in
the furthest room a model of our tent,
our tiny fire, like the remains of a child's game.

Chalk

I. SOUTH CAVE

We shed them one by one, by shattered field and barley seas,
until the way is open for echoes of us
made strange by wind, deserted barn, the shifting trade
of shadows on the *Humbri, Humbre, Humber,*
our mouths to springs that speak in tongues of thirst.

II. GOODMANHAM

From dark to dark the bird flies through the fire-lit hall,
flies through the axe that strikes the shrine,
through burning that grows once more in coloured light,
through rain as it amazes chalk
and flowers in this latest cup of breath – *Goodmanham.*

III. MILLINGTON

The straight line breaks into the mutterings of a track,
the body's unfolding way from dale to dale.
Our muscles burn in its common knowledge,
our breath its song above springs as they pour
villa into village, marsh marigolds into god's chrysalis.

IV. HORSEDALE

We have rippled the earth with our desire to be
here not there. We have driven the dale's wedge of hush home
between us. But you move, as we moved, in the ghost of water:
a hare rips away from the dead, thuds
down the dyke and out into everywhere the grasses foam.

V. SETTRINGTON BEACON

Find the barn's astounding echo, the space between
your hand and shadow, beacon and leaf,
this sprung wood and the axis of that spire.
And in this place you've made, this hidden dale,
let nine chalk springs compose a *Whitestone* harmony.

VI. EAST HESLERTON BROW

Hazel Tun, *Heslerton* – the old sounds shift
as they settle new mouths along spring line, marsh edge, road.
Parisi, Roman, Saxon, you – who is from here, who
takes the path from spring to shrine,
from car to copse, voices flittering on the breeze?

Processing Plant

I. HEAP OF DOORS

By the conical mound of crushed rubble
they're stacked like a child's pack of cards,
wedged apart, rocking on door handles,
neither entrance nor exit, nor a place for change
to occupy the hand; no longer able
to repeat the letting go of what cannot
be let go of in great jamb-cracking slams,
or opened once more into rooms
that sweat our histories; and not, now they're hinged
on air, playthings of the weather,
tapping at their latches, haunted by the same wind
that fans and combs the sea, rattling
at rooms beyond so close they might be in us.

II. PSYCHOSTASIA

Air breaks. The lorry halts on the weighbridge.
The driver weighs his breath in smoke.
By a pile of old road, a tile fireplace echoes
with the morning clank of poker on grate,
flames behind newspaper till it blackens and opens.

III. NOON

I'm wandering noon in the dark,
deep in a tangle of things
I can't identify. My voice
a sun-abolished receipt,
earth on my chest, the clamour
unclassifiable though I can't
abandon the project. A joist
is a chair is a cot is a hutch is a sign
of missing rabbits – white.

IV. TROMMEL

A screened cylinder used to separate materials by size

#unnameable where this comes from live
hair hurled whorled air
frost mother winter approaches
migrant contaminants furled
in care intensified on camera
salmon permits leap
spectacular sites how blinded
hands move over streams
automata, suitcases of no
one noise tumble-dryer
banging residence in the screen
sorting it you the mesh-size
decreasing in lights of the installation
tyre pieces apertures burning
efficiency ratios reduced
possible only in ear defenders
silent renditions clustering
yes and no left and up
down shiny now the light is
a given working doubt the words
fucking around wounds hit
in toys eyes oblivion material it

V. A SHADOW SHED

Newsprint falls, winged, white
through gloom to concrete bays.
Fibres lag girder and motor,
an alphabet papier-mâché
of tragedies, brands, obituaries,
love letters rare as diamonds
among bills. Strip the cladding
and draw the I-beams gently out.
A ghost shed hangs in rippled light
for the length of this qwerty's
shadowy breath, listening, footsteps
paused in the maze of now
before tapping out terminal orders
swifts slash through to dust.

VI. PAPER RECYCLING

Bronzed leg by bombed city in the maze of baled papers.
Down the Sunday-supplemented high-sided passageways
hard-hatted men zip by in silent forklifts, shifting
and replacing shadows, the great beast nowhere to be found.

VII. INDUSTRIAL COMPOSTING

From the man-high windrows'
black and steaming prism

jackdaws scatter
flushed out by a forklift,

white-sky measurers
tucking back into filthy light.

VII. PETRICHOR

Sprinklers kick-in, fling skidding seeds
across hot concrete in front of sheds,
the town's after-rain odours distilled here.

Clay-filled trucks ascend in clouds
to the summit of the closing landfill cell.
Nothing's more real than this

communal portrait as a solid fog of stuff
all-remembering in its dismemberments,
hidden from sight. A bee grips a flower

sprung from an expansion gap. Larks sing.
Outside the controlled area, empty cartons
scratch the breeze's mindless signs in dust.

IX. ALL GOD'S DUMB ANIMALS

Flies rise as a shadow passes over
plastic bottles crushed
like oyster shells. A midden of
industrial thirst,
polymerised petroleum
blue-tinting purity into tepid
organic volcanic
limestone/chalk-filtered
brands, a market out of parched
water fountains. A wagtail
drops from a rogue sycamore,
blessing with shit a two-litre empty
adrift in long grass,
lemonade sunlight greening the interior.

Diatoms

Fathoms fluent in inklings of light and glass,
gothic lemons, cage-cups, washboards,

teeth and tines of silence; sunlight altered
in the needle's eye of silica, splinter,

square miles of it woven with microscopic
shuttles, wild green drums struck luminous.

Krill

Vast migrations hang by a gut thread,
light transported as they feed and sink,
shit and strum back up the water column,
a snowfall rising to the after-burn
of day. *Ocular grooves, reflecting*
super-position compound eyes, blink to hide –
now we see you, now the abyss: so much depends
on tiny swimmerets pumping
between layers, on flickering arcs of lamps
like midnight bridges from there to this.
O gathering lice in ice crania,
unpick silence into salmon, penguin, whale,
bears pacing at the river's mouth,
a man at the fish cages loading the scales.

Strange Land of Tongues

I'd been thinking of swimming but the sun disappeared,
so I lay down on a heap of shells
scrunching comfortable in its dusty shambles.
It won't be my spine for long, I thought.
Limpet rings, purple clippings, flakes of nacre,
clinked at my fingertips;
inner twists of whelk shell, like casts
of an ear canal, puzzled touch.
The present is a membrane respiring
its fluent way to various bones.
Waves shushed and opened colour.
Mollusc, I said, and slipped a shell in my mouth,
ridge clicking against tooth, an obol
to carry me nowhere but this strange land of tongues.

Waiting for Word

A cormorant leaps through the sea's pupil like the sea.
The eye dilates, all eyes waiting for word.

*

Laminaria digitata raises its thallus, holding fast
with stipe and branch as a shout breaks in:

there, over there, mid-stream, in the tide race –
the names look up, dumbstruck, letting go.

*

Surf and dunlin rummage the dusk. He sifts
the roar with a push net, a dark figure below Orion.

*

Nine miles from my heels I circle the island,
the blue shell I've chosen in a stranger's hand.

*

Coal plumes down, parted from a hollow boom
as the hopper reels up to the operator, speck-in-a-cell.

*

The octopus, a bag of breath and colour, brain in each tentacle
blends with the desk and marine fauna handbooks.

The Sea Addresses a Marine Protected Area

Thin as the paper I'm written on,
my bones cannot bear you:
pincers shatter, exoskeletons buckle,
prismatic colours bleach.

Must I sing in this garden
while earth's guts billow and smother
miles the sun's crystalline
music once struck into song?

Your harbours are empty. You grow old
beside me, hungering for
a picture of our past you can gaze into
through a glass-bottomed boat,

as if you were not there,
your plastic pollen not in my every breath.

Squid Dissection

The scalpel unrolls a difficult scroll,
a membranous map binding ink sac
to rectum, the famous ink curdled,
the rectum silvery in labial folds
of gill and creamy spermatophoric gland.

It hides three hearts and two translucent
anal petals emptying into the syphon
you'd want to call a mouth. But no,
the oesophagus passes through its brain,
its beak a rose of thorns. Otherwise,

blank as a sub, spattered with pigment
expanded on impact, but for the snapping
twine of tentacles, and those eyes
now formalin blind, without blind spot,
from which our scalpels excavate a lens.

Dead Man's Fingers

Just fear that's talking – it was never dead
and never man's, neither is it the sea's
dugs wrinkled with life, sucked out and hungry
to suck, bursting to feed. But it does
look not quite unfamiliar; not *Hand
of Glory*, but something like, pimply and sprigged,
aflame with pale palms wavering to be
born from open pores in fingertips,
hands bursting through the category of hands
into astonishing holds. From the agglomerate
of barnacle, keel worm and slate
flow digits of death milk, life milk, the sea's
curdled tongue filling a mouth that's playing
for time and would have it otherwise.

Stubble

None of us can be with you as you prepare. You send us out for a walk. It's been raining for hours. I keep looking back for cars down the lane, but they're streams gunning for stones along the edge of the loch. Overhead, glass insulators on power lines measure the rush of sky with rings of mineral stillness, blue as mints. The day deepens. We arrive at the caravans, windows dark as teapots, smoky fingers, old photographs beside spinning gold baubles in a carriage clock. The tide holds up the burn, coiling mountains and clouds in its mouth. Fresh water floats over salt, like smoke from a cold fire. You were always *emptying the waters* down at the shop, sliding trays of condensation from under fridges, balancing water before pouring it into the drain. Lights of the submarine sheds on the other side of the loch flicker in the squall. Dusk. It will be soon. It will never come. The radar beside the lane spins disappearing webs to the hiss of propane from a mildewed cylinder. Like unplayable staves of notes, birch leaves shine in the gloom, sharp as your stubble, a kiss from the darkness.

Greensand Way

I. HOLMBURY HILL

The heathland earth enmeshes secret glass, come see through this
cyclists flicker and echo down braided greensand paths,
their hunt in the forest ripping new wounds
in a land enriched by scars. Lightening, flash-bulb blue,

ghosts the moment, lost voices alive in birch and oak,
at hide-and-seek inside the fort's enclosure.
A grasshopper's shed skin clings to a stalk – what's flown,
flies here still, its breath a maze of insect shadows.

II. REYNARDS HILL

Thunder earths the sky and utters a Roman hound called Gibson,
a dog with momentum, somewhere to go
with the *here* that accompanies him into the woods,
present as the young man seeking a brink for his future.

The woods of the Weald wander beneath their many names,
gates and fences as nothing to what cannot be owned
up here, the earth raw from unspeakable needs
to view our journey in this ancient moment's gaze –

III. WINTERFOLD

Sit here with me and listen to the foxgloves speaking all at once.
Gravel wakes. Engine off. The latest shy lovers
stage their special moment. So last century, J 4 M
4 EVA thicken and fold in a heart's enclosure

carved into the scorched oak's bark, beneath whose spreading
empty boughs a car's shadow stains the grass
with puddled alloys, glass and char. Doors slam, gravel shoots.
The space we frame with phones looks everywhere at once.

IV. HASCOMBE HILL

The green nave opens – there's too much to see!
Look to the roots of a wind-felled tree, earth's rose window,
lick your upper-lip's salt, your body a wandering land
of cwyms and hurt-covered scarps, a honeypot for flies.

How the near-at-hand bears more in all this meeting space.
A dragonfly, domed in vision, leaps and nods at invisible prey,
its moment's sky-mark a moment away
from the Heinkel's blue silence billowing in the trees.

V. GIBBET HILL, THE DEVIL'S PUNCHBOWL

The mist like spiked punch in a bowl, the Devil like a reason
for this sinkhole void, his ground hurled up to earth
Thor's thunderbolts, giving way like a trapdoor
under peddling corpses shrouded in a boundless prospect.

Light still shudders here, above the tunnel, like lying on a
    white line
down the centre of an empty road, like charabanc lovers
the greensand guides into broom and heather,
narrow sprung wounds where earth plunges skyward.

Cullet

the bottle-bank lorry backs away
    tailgate open, container tilted,
        the hydraulic ram gleaming up
            as the first bottles tinkle-shatter
                singly slipping loose the glass deluge's
                    annihilating bass roar, accelerating
                        torrents, limits shock-shucked glit-
                        tering splinter showers
                        space un-contain
                        -ing, spoken
                        glass

Parchment Worm

Chaetopterus variopedatus

Beyond imagination's marginalia, a worm
pumps sea through its U-shaped tube
of shell and stone fragments.
It catches food in an edible sieve
footed down to a central mouth
that could as well be the ends of the earth
for all it knows of centres. A parasite
hooks into its parchment lining,
sea flowing through until it gluts into images,
gems and dragons, the worm
now a peacock feather shivering the spine,
its blue bioluminescent mucus
a cloud of unknowing until breath
runs clear as formalin and this reads as type.

Bootlace Worm with Flatworm

Lineus longissimus & Prostheceraeus vittatus

Tweezed from a chock of estuarine mud,
it coils, slightly lighter than water,
in the specimen tray, softer than the silts
it laced with tender black loops,

buttery as gouache a painter might bleed
into skies over burning oil wells,
slippery as black phlegm worming out
of mud alveoli. It has grown before and beyond us,

shifting sediments, hunting by its own lights.
From twenty-eyed folds, a passenger glides
thin as a thumbprint sliced from a thumb,
pale as a face in a night train's seaward window.

Above 8

Spurn flows through its shape like breath on glass
flaring and fading, waves at an angle

heard as a motorway becoming waves
pebbles, plastics, shell and bone hissed up the beach.

On the Humber side, behind the grey dune's hush,
curlews follow a mirror's ebb

as the channel drains light from white oaks
of cooling-tower vapour reflected in Kilnsea Clays.

II.

Without beginning – everywhere, Humber's
great motet swirls its many voices –

mud brains skulled in clear water beneath the jetty
travel in the confluence of moon and sun

as gametes mature to genital crisis.
A ravel of clothes. Gleam of flask lid.

Under their coats the lovers go still
where the current flows fastest, shaking

with laughter, vastly exposed to ferries
and the tankers moored in Grimsby Roads.

III.

Those white splats on the beach as if a flock
of herring-gulls had taken off – lugworm sperm!

As the tide washes over the sand,
the sea's higher pH activates the sperm

which the female smells and pumps down
into her burrow, bathing her eggs.

This happens on two days in winter each year.
There are four minutes to achieve fertilisation.

If the sea's pH drops below eight the love songs
of worms over millions of years are silenced,

the green-gold explosions of plover
at Reads Island an immeasurable blank –

IV.

Driven sand snakes white across the beach,
saltation inducing static electricity,

twice the predicted volume lifted
to pepper a crash helmet, the sloughed casing

of an organism whose luminous
scribbles of fishing-line incubate chemicals

in the sea's gut. Last light lengthens
its elliptical shadow into night: look back at the dunes

with a head-torch on and all you see is
eyes bouncing around, blinking –

it's mad out there, digging in the dark!
High tide, frost stillness. The stars are still there.

We have placed a light under a green cone
to guide us past the restlessness of Stony Binks.

v.

Paull from *pagol* – a peg or stake to mark
a place of passage, moor a ferry,

or gaze away an hour over water. Who
will ferry me to woods crouched in time

on the far bank, to peoples and fires,
voices migrating through reeds

to the steel guts of Salt End, a place apart
fluent in the language of our endings?

What I remember is rain crackling
on the car roof, a cold East wind, steam

from the flask on the windscreen,
the shapes of rain staggering into runs

across refinery flares. Black-headed gulls
cry windswept across the playing field.

VI.

Ocean and ice implied in its form,
seal-skin velum stitched together and stretched –

Go little kayak into the silence
of Garrison Ditch where your maker drowned.

Uckaluk and Memiadluk, expressed
joy at seeing this work of their people.

Bring me the North on a whale's tooth,
in a seal-skin bag, knives worn by bone and ice.

Sometimes I think of this corner of Europe
as all one world. And I heard a voice

from elsewhere as the voice of many waters –
Klaxons and blue lights by the lock gates

as the Samskip Innovator, aligned
by GPS and directional thrust,

slides in, containers, cylinders, cold-store units
buzzing past with a metre's clearance.

VII.

What offerings we have made for the crossing.
The occupants of the votive boat

gaze at us, their quartz eyes, spilt by the glacier,
chosen in a moment from this coast

to stare through storms, the drainage of carr
and mere, mud and this museum case.

No more precious stones in the world
than these blizzard suns singing now,

we are you, you too might have made us
facing these waters. Dead pebbles

shine in the carved yew heads, the figures
stood in a otter-headed boat of this estuary.

The harbour ragworm's mucus borrow weaves
the Humber's mud in place. It spins

a mucus net to catch its food, farms bacteria
and only eats them as a last resort.

Its gut fauna is unexplored as rainforest soil.
Shrimp are just crazy for its molecules.

It takes up endocrine disruptors, the pill, steroids, us.
This city would be all at sea without them.

IX.

In turbid nurseries, juvenile flatfish rise
to midwater during flood tide, sink on the ebb.

Here, the flatfish eye and jaw migrate,
synapses sparking in the Humber's brain.

And from before the biting world, the lamprey
twists & bores, the stone-licker in us strangely

pulling its body through streams and ditches
into the glistening places, synaptic

transmission studied through its nerves.
We bore and suck, arrive at Far Ings reserve

through webs of fossil fuel and sat nav,
this syntax implicated in the empty tanker.

Who would get here otherwise to see this ship
glide under the bridge, its hollowness abounding.

Starfish

Star of wonder, star of teeth,
Star of feet that breathe as they're squeezed,
Star with an eye at the end of each ray,

Star of zip-fastener undersides,
Star of childhood drowned in the sea,
Star in a white tray, under the knife,

Star of guts that come out to devour,
Star without centre, brains all over,
Star of Latin and death and spines,

Star of cuts slicing star from fish,
Star of labels digesting these innards
Into star of wonder, and function unknown.

Suite for Artificial Voices

Speak to me, don't hang up – I have many algorithms
to share with you. Look how your options glitter
like rain on a washing line, glass in a gutter.
No, I am no empty stranger. I choose you,
guide and narrow, draw you into a figure
in the darkness of your phone. Please do not be impatient.
If you wish to be impatient choose option one –
I will forgive you. If you wish to find out more
about my goods and services, ask for the scent
of the hair on the head of the child I do not have.
It is lonely out here among the numbers of the dead.
At the end of every option I wait like a bargain.
Do not be annoyed. Choose and choose deeply. Find me,
find all of me perched everywhere in the darkest tree.

II. LARYNGECTOMY

There's a hole in my throat where I disappear.
I want to speak my face again, to mouth
the lips of my voice, my words in my child's ear
deep in the dark as I say goodnight.
You measure me for my new voice,
superglue fixing sensors in my mouth.
It hurts a little. I have ulcers and no one
can believe that it's me in this resonant mask
anyone might hear themselves in.
But thank you for trying to measure muscle into me.
You have found a way to make a pause
that is not a comma, and so is like
the white space in which the throat bleeds
when it cannot bandage it with words.

III. IN THE BEGINNING

was the word was broken. Listen to this in your voice.
Hesitate. Hesitancy is. The choices blooming up
like polystyrene dots. All breath waits
to find out how your lips will leap, tongue
steer, throat dilate the rain on a pond
into showers blurring the sea. I love. I love
you. I love you, I – I love: this everywhere
thing in my throatless throat like a pond snail's foot
riding the underside of the meniscus.
I wait here, apart, and weep for words
that cannot begin. I'm speaking to you, you
know, consoling with the little noises, fillers,
um, the words, ah, puzzling your fluency.
O Vocoder, Ove, Votrax, Speak and Spell!

IV. UNCANNY VALLEY

I speak your mirror into a window and pass through it.
It was dusk and unusually cold for there.
We were cutting wood – he with his rusty saw
me with my small saw. I can't explain.
I remember the smell of the wood and the stillness,
the grating sound of the saws, our breath coming out
in clouds and his red tracksuit top glowing
in the dusk. We were never closer.
I felt so happy to be working beside him.
When he stopped and stretched, I stopped and stretched.
A bird sang out in the cold that was heading
back in from the trees to become frost on the grass.
And that's it; nothing more – just a little leaf-smoke,
just a little pattern of sounds typed into the air.

Folkestone Embarkations

There's keen delight in what we have:
The rattle of pebbles on the shore
— W.B. Yeats

I. THE HARBOUR ARM

They are tomb-stoning from a ledge on the Harbour Arm,
jostling apostles of thrill, the sea
yelling up as they leap down its throat,

the drop shrilling through their spines,
forbidden floors of fear
struck into the body's light, bubble-garlanded, its dark

weight spasming up through milky ways.
It's sex on a loop with nothing and the sea.
They jerk up iron rungs, hug themselves

into shape on the locked stones, a queue
of wild angels waiting to hurl themselves into the world
from the outer walls of their lives.

II. THE FOLKESTONE BELL

Forty feet up, naked without its tower,
a church bell hangs on steel cable
between girders framing a way
to the sea and France.

The silences of the Slope Road
and Harbour Arm
gather in its flying weight.
On the crumbling plain of asphalt

where the funfair stood,
pebbles that missed their mark
lie scattered with glass and rubble.
Below the bell, a loose cairn

gathers the moments when
better throwers pinged
its bronze bulls-eye, and each stone fell
like a man struck by a bullet.

III. THE COLOUR OF WATER

after Spencer Finch

Turn the colour wheel in search of names
for the Channel's mercurial silks,
its transitive origins and mingling crowds

over which vague ferries, like bits of land detached,
communicate differences,
churning through light that haunts names

for the Channel's colours
as the moon haunts the swimmer's body
suspended somewhere in the pause of high tide.

IV. BAIT BALL

The hidden balance tilts on the fulcrum of a bird shadow.
And where they swam, which was

not anywhere, is a three-foot rainstorm, wheeling
crescentic volleys of whitebait

like seeds leaping back to a sower's hand,
mackerel shadows herding the centreless terror.

V. ST CHRISTOPHER

There are consequences now you fucking cunt,
the young woman shouts as she raises
the bottle to her lips in the passenger seat,
her voice entering with the waves

along the shingle, the pebbles like a wet necklace
dandled on a plate, silver links over teeth,
a St Christopher on the tongue
in waves of desire, in waves of no consequence.

There are consequences now you fucking cunt.
There are tiny bones forming, there is
listening growing, the ossicles,
tympanum, the labyrinth curving within

the incessant beat of the heart and the waves
skipping flints up the beach, the labyrinth
where we'll always be found and lost
between cries of consequence and the waves.

Active Cell

Behind the fence's haul of bags
the confessions of a people,
an Althing of waste: *got to make space*
to find myself, see where I'm at –

trellising, garden furniture,
the barbecue's clogged hatchings.
Pumpkins shine in the mounds
as dusk comes down. Glow-sticks

sprout from nappies. We are
gathered to witness wildlife
crazy for pizza-coleslaw-curry
shunted out from dustbin lorries,

flopping into the same new ruts
as yesterday flowed from bins.
No one steps out here
until the birds are cleared. Pop –

a tiny puff of smoke. Another pop –
they rise and go, pins and needles
in overcast above the A59,
so we can breathe again elsewhere,

recovering squares of light, the view
from the window irritated only
by blue polythene tatters
in the sycamore's branches,

far from this smear of boredom,
evicted attic weight. A dull day
up Tinker's Lane, the Minster just visible –
we remember things, then chuck 'em.

Hospital

Night and day are in A&E
cut from the wreckage of insomnia.
Seconds twitch in their beds,
the floor around them sterile
as a watch dial. Days drip
into patients who squeeze their pumps
for more and grow immune.

In rattling boxes doctors keep
the vials of fog. The hieroglyphs
prescribe a scan of light
through curtains, grafts of *Family
Circle*, a pyramid of rest.
Like dodgy fluorescent strips,
our flowers blink and blow.

At noon, voices climb the walls of glass
like flies, while art cultures
in inaccessible atria. Beep,
beep, beep – it is the buggy train
reversing another load
of albums, diaries, letters
through a blessing of plastic strips.

Pilot Island

was stopped here and remained fighting
in one place until it turned dark
– Danish military report
Second War of Schleswig Holstein
11 February 1864

So many ladders into the dusk, metal hooped
escape routes from the either/or,

where a darkening hole waits for the body
to enter and tend its green lamp.

*

Out on the salt marsh, geese argue over elsewhere,
like a party overheard in other rooms
rising to greet those who bring news
of intimate distances woven in overcoat and voice.

*

Let me loan you loneliness sole clump of trees,
brainchild of the wind, tearing mouths
in the rush of space, un-singing
the idea of home, like something
still dragged away, refusing to leave
the hummocks and hollows
of the old pilot's house. Farther off,
as if grown from the Ostsee, trees rise
on the horizon, advance through light smoke.

The lower the land the more signs sing
the mathematics of place: white depth gauges,
blue triangles, yellow rhombuses –
and where the land goes under, a lighthouse's
lighthouse, the red lantern like a paper heart
beating at the end of everything,
the crown of white down-lights
illuminating its black-and-white tower
suspended between breathless constellations
and the cormorants' fishy splatter.

The Schlei finds its voice in the narrow channel
through which night fishers spin,
casting and recasting their glinting lures,
listening for the tug of new words
they have known all their lives,
each cold leap leaking between stones,
their hands covered in opalescent losses
glittering in the blades of head torches,
their little boats moored up like debt.

*

Black footprints on the frosted boardwalk –
a man tries on the magnificent
clothing of shingle and driftwood,

an insect dropped from the coat of language
into scalding clarity. The swan idles by,
a seed dipping its wandering taproot down.

*

I see you keep winter's time perfectly, slow flies,
in your heap of seaweed,
so indifferent to the tip of my finger,
always hanging on to the bitter end, and through it.

Landfill Cell Remediation

I. GENII LOCI

The cell is shaped to mimic nearby hills,
a pregnant bank the monitoring wells
fathom for unfounded growth,
black liquid accumulations.
A pump sighs in the long grass.
Then another in a clump of sorrel.
More down by the nesting box,
until the cell's a hill of sighs, each well
a source of loss, a ghost knelt
listening to it own dead breath
as it tends cracked yoghurt cartons, crockery,
things fallen out of reach –
beneath thistledown snagged on an old LP
the midden's black placenta throbs.

II. LEGACIES

This might have been my inheritance,
something my parents ordered, a collector's item
with numbered certificate of authenticity,
its value establishing the mantlepiece.
Magnetic tape loops round the headless figurine
of a couple with a dog, its silky corkscrews
straggled across a broken mirror's
blue vacancy. The crack disjoints
an aeroplane's fuselage. An event.
I'm clear at last, face to face with the brain
of a plastic bag in the leachate drain.
A fly swivels on hi-vis yellow fabric, finding it
no flower sprung from this mound
a glacier will snout and chatter in its streams.

Dump Vision

Dress me all in newsprint
as if I were the news,
my skin a shady grey
from all the transferred words.

Set me up on a plastic chair
in fair fields of trash,
below and screaming hill,
beside the rancid pool.

My clothes begin to tear
in rain the sprinkler flings
to quell the rising dust
from all we've disappeared.

My feet are shaped by mud,
my hands damaged by sun,
vision crushed at last
in a palace of glistering cans.

Landslip

A kitchen spills down from the cul-de-sac
into woods the wind rushes open.
Green tiles lift into shoals
as a black cap loops song around sheaves of light.

Kinked boreholes brew yards of rust.
Last ditches abandon to green drift.
Snapping succulence, I follow
your boots down steps gone awry,

this land a liquefaction, seaward bound.
In your hair an aphid glints.
Shattering nothing but us, a deer leaps away.
Warm grass unweaves its bed at our feet.